Hidden Motion

poems by

Matthew James Babcock

Finishing Line Press
Georgetown, Kentucky

Hidden Motion

Thanks

To the editors at *Juxtaprose* for giving "What Is a Crow?" the Juxtaprose
        Poetry Prize
To Liz, Alexander, David, Diane, Bethany, and the Cabin in Boise
To Constance and Kathleen at *Gyroscope Review* for making me poet of the
        day during National Poetry Month

Publisher: Leah Huete de Maines
Editor: Christen Kincaid
Cover Art and Design: Scott Samuelson
Author Photo: Matthew James Babcock

Order online: www.finishinglinepress.com
        also available on amazon.com

Author inquiries and mail orders:
Finishing Line Press
P. O. Box 1626
Georgetown, Kentucky 40324
U. S. A.

Table of Contents

III. RARE MEASURE

IV. FIRST ECHO

for my boy and girls
all mystery, all life, all motion

And this inner vision, what is its operation?

—Plotinus

I

SPARE GOLD

What Is a Magpie?

after Susan Elizabeth Howe's "What Is a Grackle?"

Jocular old boxer, jockey swaggering
in patched black and white satin,
raucous uncle with the bluesy squawk

of a young Joe Cocker.
No jackdaw, no Australian butcherbird—
too loose. Glib opportunist with a cry

like a hacksaw, glossy spin doctor
drag racing cops, goosing the throttle,
snoozing in superhero silks.

Behold the bruised lover. Balloon vendor
snagging stragglers at the Job's
Daughters Dance in used blue tuxedo.

Magpies laugh at their own gaffs,
dirty jokes rolling like boxcars through
family gatherings. From junkyard jukeboxes

they airlift in the biker jackets of drifters,
sling breezy news from six-shooters—
titter, gawk, chaffer, shmooze, wink and gargle—

proof you come back as the real you.
Boozed up, bulletproof smile, zoot suit
the sheen of a cheap razor.

Cheeky *Pica pica* flubbing Latin and Greek,
Mark Twain in clownish doctoral gowns,
shoebox of medals rubbed smooth. *You choose,*

they warble, lollygagging in long lines
to haggle for the bargain bauble. *In every puddle*
shines a miracle. Every mile a free meal.
You can never take too many bows.

Wisdom of the Magpie

the six maxims

What is every February moon
but the amber in your eye?

The footloose goose cruises in the caboose.

Some days only you can take the snake
out of the snake oil.

Sinister sisters: punch clock and prescription.

Roam rhymes with home rhymes with shalom
rhymes with Om rhymes with . . .

Brood tomorrow.

What Is a Crow?

after Susan Elizabeth Howe's "What Is a Grackle?"

In fours, the horsemen who took
Becket's skull for a punchbowl,
hunched on a whip of birch to swab swords

athwart a March sky like a kingdom
coming apart. Solo: sullen sniper.
Craven cousin to the raven,

toadie to buzzard, suckled on biohazard
in the trailer of a spavined carnival barker.
Crows darken darker. They breathe malice

then backpedal. Scofflaws of schoolyard brawl
and skedaddle. Who looms more
like the gargoyle? Who leers, whose art

is to startle with the velvet swoosh
of stealth bomber in bad weather, as welcome
as the slap of broken windshield wiper,

as bridesmaid is to bookie and bird to viper?
X-ray's no shocker: stunted bones,
gizzard of aborted sonnets, heart a licorice tart.

Skywriting at midnight across garbled clouds,
the cicatrix of the moon, five spells dulled
to doggerel—gripe, stutter, croak, seethe, mumble.

A deft snatch at Bob Cratchit's coal.
A sneer for the hatchet job that sends a friend
the way of Lear's fool. *I am mayhem,*

they drawl, dimming parlor lights
until wine goblets sparkle. *I am the ancient eyes.*
The oddball shuffle. Hooked tool prying open young souls.
Watch your daughter.

Magic of the Crow

the five chants

I am the flying V in villain. The Immortal Brotherhood
of the Divine Presumption.

I am the cold candle in the hand of vagabond and vandal.

I am on tiptoes to see the chopping block, the butler
laughing at the sprained ankle.

I am sickle and switchblade, tourniquet and turncoat.
Eclipse and cliff, the click of latch and slipped disc.

I am the slither of lascivious drool under the Druidic hood.
I am the hurt you crave. The pain of good.

What Is a Flamingo?

after Susan Elizabeth Howe's "What Is a Grackle?"

Spindly dandies in the pink of youth,
jostling for seats in Drury Lane's
priciest boxes. Cotton candy for foxes.

Entering through exits, the clueless slue-foot
doofus, a tangle of angles, gangly beatnik
banging bongos. Flamingos lap the hype,

guffaw google-eyed at sitcom stereotypes.
But what flavors! What hues!
Plumage from bubble gum to mango,

from champagne to the dyed hair
of the guy in Oingo Boingo.
All foofaraw and fandango, something daffy

and strawberry taffy in this pencil-necked,
knock-kneed Theater of the Absurd.
Pure gringo, tutti frutti galoot, goofball roommate

who intrudes—oops!—while you're making out
on the couch, your girlfriend's tangy
lip gloss, your tongues doing a tango.

Dorkier than storks. Bigger scoop shovels
than spoonbills or herons, jiving on juice
jazzier than Django, a beak like Ringo!

Catch phrases hatch from the Bahamas to Peru—
hoot, chortle, burp and guzzle. Footloose souls
staining the sky over the Congo. *Senoritas!*

they whistle from rented sports coupes,
toupées askew. *Come, speak
to me love's Lingo Franco! Migrating my way?
The interior's all plush. Try not to blush.*

Pick-up Lines of the Flamingo

the four clichés

Excuse me, is this front lawn taken?

Hold still, I think you have something in your ibis.

Hope you don't mind me saying, but we could make beautiful mudflat together. Wait, I know I have the body of a bass clarinet, but we could still have great sax.

Bingo!

What Is a Pelican?

after Susan Elizabeth Howe's "What Is a Grackle?"

From the ground, a particle wave
crossing humid noon. Stern sage
in repose among the moorings,

tourists murmuring concessions
into coffee cups. In motion,
a Da Vinci diagram streaming

in daydream stage. Pelicans unfurl
more than ascend, launch
like unbound manuscripts

hurled into headwinds. Their wingspans
plane edges from storms.
Presume a uniform procession,

and they assume more roles
than the red horizon holds:
staunch reformer, serene wingman,

ascetic in the senate of sky,
outfitted with the evolutionary wonder
of gold cutlass and swag bag,

the endless sunrise in the mage's eye.
Adopt one as cosmic consort,
or anoint your dozing confessor.

Recall the stately white male scarcely
audible on the mirror lake—
lull, charm, and descant: *Stay stoic,*

came the telepathic trace. *You are
the marble before the temple. Always
sculptor and sculpture in the air,
the everlasting space spanning here and there.*

Philosophy of the Pelican

the three creeds

The needless thought ever encumbers.

The seedless heart never numbers.

The heedless soul forever slumbers.

Maundy Thursday

Straightway, the long winter flees
  the grazed landscape of our faces.
A new heat illuminates the gritty
  sidestreets behind Ard's Paint & Glass.
In Lhasa, the firebombs of March
  blossom from cracked pavement.
Protestors slalom through bronze monks
  to peel sheets of wrinkled steel
from shopfronts. A ragged vet pedals
  Hungry Please Help on a child's buggy
crammed with camos and canned peaches
  through an American town from which
four generations have not strayed.
  The revolutions of spring summon us
to a vagabond supper of last days.
  Shrouds of drizzle sustain their gray
betrayal then blow the sky to rags
  and bathe a republic of refugees
in gasoline dusk. Swallows riot around
  yellow fire hydrants. Slow cyclones
of crows settle the solace of Tibet
  on elementary schools and scuttle
rare coins of dirty ice down rain gutters.
  Dissidents in the capital city
and the single mother who whips
  a chocolate cashier smock from
her waist outside The Cash Store halt
  at curbside, unsure if they will stay
and fight. The cold breath of Judas
  blows grocery receipts across parking lots.
The savory smoke of summer troubles
  what the masses believe. Imperial
day restrains the rabble it urges to leave.

In Keeping

In keeping with doctrines and myths
of immortality, I haven't banished
from the urban thoroughfare of my gray
memory the girl who between frail fists
carried a grimy paper cup of wishes.

On a Dublin street she begged for change.
The day drove a pandemonium of souls
east and west through the city's mixed forge
of carbon sunrise. Every way, grungy
pavement rang with crusades of smoky scowls.

My English pound clinked her coins.
I spun, and she pursued, suddenly alive,
her spate of scattershot narrative
slicing the moist air to pennants of pain:
starving brother, no bus fare, chips and gravy.

Two more coins. Then, seeing I'd been tricked
I barked a reproof. Nimble rodent,
she bolted through seams of human traffic,
gums bleeding, cheeks smudges of smog.
Her glance embossed the metal of the moment.

I was running then, fugitive of summer,
before I knew you. Waylaid in the decay
of a generous time, I hadn't dared
to flee the hour that steals the foundling's pay,
to give all in keeping the penny of fire,

to hoard the tarnished suns that appear
to scavenge the spare gold of a second day.

We Are a Country

of crucifixes made of white PVC pipe
stabbed in the dirt at roadside,
of chintzy pink pinwheels, brass urns
and button-eyed teddy bears
with purple tummies, prayer beads
and peace symbol pillows heaped at the foot
of pallet slats nailed into crosses
at the summit of Malad Pass,
shrines of black-eyed Susans
and supermarket mums shining
in September sun like boutounnières of blood,
of makeshift memorials on that last
dangerous curve after Castle Rock
on Highway Twenty as you approach
Mountain Home so Dave
or Emilio or Duffy can know
we think of them even though
they didn't think of themselves,
a country of vigils without vigilance,
of sideswipe and broadside and jackknife
and midnight pile-up of weekend pilgrims
who mark disaster then wheel around
and overshoot the same turn,
unlike Tim Goodale, who, hearing of
Shoshoni hostiles to the south
near Massacre Rocks, steered over
a thousand wagons in safe passage
across miles of wild wasteland to the northeast,
one thinking man's quest still carved
in ruts through the sagebrush
and lava rock in a country
of rubbernecker roadkill and rumble strips,
of gin rummy and crash test dummies
for gods, for the spilled radiator fluid
of dreamy patriots, for bits of glass
twinkling in the spacious everlasting splendor
of shattered windshield skies.

We Are a World

of little aristocrats who won't make
our own pizzas, who demand
that groceries and grinders be delivered
to palazzos someone else designed,
a world of self-styled gentry
dependent on the resplendence
of seamstresses in the Phillipines,
armies and navies and marines to guard
garages of grizzled car mechanic
gurus, math tutors in imported shoes
and business suits woven on
computerized looms, of truancy officers
reading robo-journalism and stopping
after work to fetch birthday cakes
encased in orange icing, brains
that once calculated bar tabs
and bank balances, vestigial arms once
good for rolling down car windows,
soldiers flying armed drones
from home, presidents on the phone
with pollsters, hiring out and hitchhiking
on the hope of hitmen and hairdressers,
surrogate mothers and sperm banks,
of remoras and rickshaws and rental cars
and rope tows and refugees
stowing away in airline luggage holds,
mooching roomies, endless taxis
of the taxed, life coaches flushing
cockroaches from designer glassware
fired in distant forges, dukes and duchesses
of the Yellow Pages, everyone a sage
and no one sure where to turn
in this New World On Back Order,
of hierarchies and networks and outreach
and late returns, borrowed livers
and kidneys and artificial hearts beating
in our bodies, fighting to preserve life
on a planet none of us made.

Home Movies

In a water-stained shoebox
in a padlocked storage unit in Twin Falls,
my father, still a young man,
bounds like a model of modern dance
around our grainy backyard
on Sunnyside Avenue in Salt Lake City,
slashing at frantic mobs of cabbage moths
with a hand-made net, as if
slicing his scimitar of a thousand Junes
through the first of many summers
to vanish too soon under the acetate sky.
My mother tries to steady 1973,
wonders where she left the manual
to our masque. In the dark room
of small histories, the scene gets labeled
"Day Without Script," part Buster Keaton,
part comic safari, armed, as we are,
with lame apparatus of broom handles,
hooped clothes hangers, and flimsy pillowcases
that billow like the breath of butterflies.
Return, heart, to when you were
the only lens. Spirit, the crackling soundtrack.
These Super 8 dreams pin me
spread-eagle to the shade of willow trees,
millimeters from the morphology
of my dad's muttonchops, vanilla flare-legs,
and purple paisley shirt with drawstrings
criss-crossing a triangle patch
of chest fuzz. On cue, he crouches
behind a picnic table, springs up, and takes
a wild swing at heaven, then peeks in
at the microscopic scales on the wings
of my unborn brother and sister.
The frame skips. The end slips free of the reel.
A shaky hand pitches us into the great
compound eye of the sun, bleaching the cyan
from our yellow afternoons, the magenta

from our laughter, souls over-exposed,
fingers shiny with the dust of a robust hatch
of what we never tire of chasing but never catch.

The Dogs of Sligo

The place that has really influenced my life the most is Sligo. There used to be two dogs there—one smooth-haired, one curly—I used to follow them all day long. I knew all their occupations, when they hunted for rats, and when they went to the rabbit warren. They taught me to dream, maybe. Since then I follow my thoughts as I then followed the two dogs—the smooth and the curly—wherever they lead me
—Yeats, Letter to Katharine Tynan

The dogs of Sligo rally like a dark
tribe of roustabouts where my Dodge Stratus
cracks seventy thousand miles. Lanky, stark,
they are ambassadors to the solstice,

the rogue December night on which I drive
through a stretch of exurbia. Steamy
tongues pink and flaccid, their ragged grins woof
the madman's silver oath of anomie.

They are the earth's urge to roam, one curly,
one straight-haired. From their dank, lice-ridden coats
and grizzled jaws wafts the hurly-burly
of mussel and seaweed stew that wrasse boats

on Donegal Bay ferry through like dreams.
The way they lope with the black Labrador
in maroon collar that skids through the beams
of my weak headlights suddenly makes clear

the mechanics of body and spirit—
the thing I never seem to get quite right.
Like a dog racing its fleet silhouette.
Like trying to track black dog in black night.

Saturday, we knew another child grew
in you at Henderson Funeral Home.
Untrained, we assembled with a stray zoo
of uncles and mongrel cousins, solemn

as apology, at the church in which
Margaret, my dad's mother, lay. Some drawled
tributes, lapped tears. Soft ears and whiskers twitched.
Horns on the highway yelped. Door hinges growled.

Did the soul of our pup, as thin as scum
on the water in a slop-crusted dish
in the garage, pass my gentle grandmum
on the way down—a nuzzle to the crotch

in greeting, a frisky nip at the hams?
What is spirit but a howl, the hunger
to retrieve? When the leash snaps, do we scram,
a kennel released, barking at strangers,

snapping at the wheels of the drab carriage?
Or sniff the rank backwater for crabs, dredge
noses in tide pools, muzzles caked with sand?
Do we fade or return to run the strand?

Running in New Hope

Stillness surges. Turn after turn
the burned world unrolls
gold corridors of corn. Light is
born. Quills of day impale
the damp sway of tigerlilies.
NO TRESPASSING signs unravel
the way to the old mill wheel.
Curiosities multiply. Nailed to a tree:
a toboggan christened "Swan."
Arrested in air, a sprained
blue jay windmill. Maple leaves
glow like fresh gashes
under a sky as gray as gravel.
The human domain invades.
Goldenrod frills the footpath
Charles Kellogg trod in another century.
Yellow bombs streak the rusty flight
of warfare across abandoned
cargo holds from Shay's of Dansville.
A man who won't wave back
enters the museum of his motions.
On the return, bold battlements
of clouds mold bolts of sun.
Monarch butterflies trade flames.
Breezes of mint skim power
from Queen Anne's lace and settle bees
in the ruins of the hour.

Running at Trearddur Bay

All ghosts. The wavering gull
with a notch in its sooty wing,
chuckling like a philosopher
aloft on some truth you should know.
Your stuttering blood.
The slipstream of your steps
drifting from echo to eclipse,
slow quick slow. On your lips
a gloss of salty mist
finer than unwritten hymns.
One blundering sky. The underbelly
of thunder, a gray language
as vast as the last unknown throat
to erode the standing stones
of its vowels. An orange tennis ball
stamped with a paw print,
dropped in sloppy sand to soak
in tide pools of lost momentum,
a blazing globe poised to roll
with all living motion from
this coastal arc of turbulence,
the black crags blanketed
in chaos of bladderwrack, the homes
on the headland like exposed bone,
reaching as far as you can alone.

Running in Amherst

Nineteen golds unravel
red maple canopies.
Dormant sparks of stone
ignite two centuries.

Trajectories of daylight
collide with fossil sound.
Oak and jigsaw sycamore
electrify the ground.

Spurs of granite shadow
slow like mossy cogs.
Glanced peripheries elude
ephemerae of frogs.

Mallard incandescence
strafes cloud curvature.
Oriole cataclysm
annihilates the air.

Strikes of yellow solitude,
birch echo residue,
from Mill River to Fort Juniper
clamor in the blue.

Forge maxims of commotion.
Ascend mist caravan.
Stand within the slipstream
to parallel the sun.

Sixteena

I loped country miles for Coach Tim Dunne.
The Bird Farm Road paced a dusty forever.
My phaeton was a '66 Karmann Ghia—
corroded cables, no muffler, all primer and thunder.
On Garfield, the water tower's scorched graffiti
sifted oracles of August through alfalfa chaff.

The Hofbräuhaus clobbered me, elbow and shove.
I bawled Climax Blues Band. I read John Donne.
Robyn was my Penelope. Suzanne: Nefertiti.
I lived for sagebrush, saxifrage, for rimrock, for river.
Nightly, dusk shrank my bland bones to tinder.
The brisk spark of morning ignited cold Gaia.

My mother and father grew gray and grayer.
I measured the day to the magpie's chaffer,
lawn mower, garden shed, gas can, paint thinner.
My friends got drunk at the Bruneau Dunes.
We flouted death's flurries with laughter, for never
would we ever furnish grave forty, grave fifty.

Shame was barbed wire. Love, zero gravity.
My older brother dated a girl named Gina.
I burned for Traci and Kris like blood in a fever.
The shadows in my room would wheel and chafe.
I tapped out, overshot, quartered off, hunkered down.
I scoured the IGA meat saw, hands red and tender.

March potato ruts whitened to windswept tundra.
Dust devils churned brittle hay bale confetti.
Roadside pheasants shook chain mail of dawn.
Sprinkler pipes chanted *The Bhagavad Gita.*
Barrow pits hoarded sheep carcass and crankshaft.
The way lay horizons off, too far over.

Lisa proposed a tryst. I thanked her for her offer.
Sleep took its text from the interstate tantra.

Jen kissed a shaggy senior with opaline Chevy
after she kissed me in our *Così fan tutte.*
My curriculum: the law of average, geo-
graphy of loss, history of a life undone.

Gee, uh. Forever gets blown to thunder and chaff.
The slow passage paints traces of faded graffiti.
The long race commences the day it is done.

To All Abandoned Cars

You have comforted me these forty years.
When I haven't looked, you've been parked
nearby—outside the Moose Lodge
after summer gymnastics camp,
before my shift at Bob's IGA, behind
our tour bus in Belfast. This morning,
you are a crippled Chevette
with North Carolina plates, nosing the curb
near the carousel that workmen
in black-and-white photos transported
from Tonawanda and, piece-by piece, rebuilt
in the purple darkness of Porter Park.
Beyond June's moody portrait
of dry cleaners and stray golden retrievers,
you inhabit the wastrel hide
of an avocado Ford Bronco on the offramp
to the Camas Bird Refuge. Rust flowers
on the grin of your rear bumper.
A warning sticker heats a square
of fluorescent orange on your
passenger-side window. Anecdote and allegory,
you allay fears about raising children
in the modern world and the threat
of meaninglessness. The radio warbles
on Barber and his "knockout," *Adagio for Strings.*
There is no death, says your presence.
Only stages of waiting before deliverance.
All my life, your shape shifting
has revealed the truth of The One in The Many—
the Volkswagen outside St. Luke's
the day I was born, the Brat at Paul's Market
that endless afternoon after graduation,
the stripped blue Civic in Mountain Green
on the way to my sister's reception.
You have been and always will be Everycar.
With your ironic badge of luminescent gold
or hot cherry chanting VIOLATION

or FINAL NOTICE. Your morality play
is the road. Your philosophy: surrender to arrive.
Don't leave me now. I'm still learning to drive.

Cruise Poem

I'd never known the full force of ginger
till you ate a root from your won ton soup
in the Seven Seas Dining Room. Later,
I tasted that woody spice down the slope
of your back when we folded together
like oceans after torch singer Karen
Saunders in the Stardust Lounge, fair weather,

and cocktails and calypso on deck nine.
Seven days, a rigor of idleness:
Cancún hawkers, the sun a scalloped shell,
daily shuffleboard tourney at four plus
chit chat with the rich Houston clientele,
snorkeling through yellow-tailed snapper deep
into blue afternoon on Roatan

in molten sapphire bays as clear as sleep,
the heat a rare medallion on your skin.
And the souvenir smuggled home with me—
those nets of ginger scent cast in our room
as if your pores had breathed a recipe
for something more solid than the Tulum
ruins. On day five, off the starboard rail

flying fish broke the surface, skimming for
the Caribbean sun as if to sail
for miles, clipped the waves like silver dollars.
Love's evolution, I wanted to say—
I pointed, you said you didn't see, *Where?*—
isn't a matter of why some breeds fly
but when to look, how long you have to stare.

The Last Time

I drove to Utah
tributaries of tar softened seams
in parking lots like erratic maps
of every broken thing.
People dozed behind closed
payday loan and soup and sandwich
places, the slow explosions
of their bodies muffled
in the stalled green
and dazed blue of wounded cars.
Traffic raced like blood cells
in a fever. Spring snow
crowned the astounding mountains.
A computer thanked me
and coughed out six cents change
at the store where I bought
paper to write this. The world
warmed when I went walking
with the golden slaughter
of dandelions on the grassy verge
of the parkway. Pansies
brandished the purple of gladiators.
Opening plum blossoms threw
body blows at ozone.
Commuters shot me strange looks
because I wore sandals in April,
a choice to please
my subconscious voice, which
for me is the cheerful woman
with curly silver hair
and cherry cardigan who sits
in her son's auto dealership
and calls names all day
into a scratchy intercom
so she has something to keep
her busy, startling me from

the used magazines of my dreams,
asking, *When was the last time*
your feet came close to touching the earth?

Last Day

To your eyes the glare of morning
cascades on Madison Junior High School
like the shattered glass case
of all the gold trophies ever won
in the Worldwide Tournament of Hurt.
You drop off your daughter
and she gambols among eighth graders
across wet grass, a fluid feat
of decadence in a masque
of merry chances. The boys and girls
gleefully swing red yearbooks
in vinyl slipcovers like minor deities
wielding glittering bucklers
against the bright stains of age.
Too swift to counter or clock, today
becomes the day you wonder how the girls
who were as old as she is now
looked like sumptuous Amazons,
always blowing up your body like a gland
when they brushed against you
to clank a quarter in Phil Collins,
always kickstarting the blue promenade
of your breath into a calamity
of mad crusades. Then you stood
in the uncertain architecture of your blood,
already amazed at the dances of desire,
believing the rumors could be true
about body and spirit, the two
who everyone said would always be a couple
but who suddenly split up
on the last day before summer break
and move away to distant towns,
no more substantial than the changes
in phases of daylight, no more sure
than the signatures of hundreds of friends.

On the Last Day of the Mayan Calendar

A van of modern mystics, we migrate
south, our medicine to drain
the drowsy blood of December
from our heels and swoon under
the hoodoo skies of Nevada.
We speak of the end of the world
like giddy girl scouts eager
to leap from the crumbling tower
of this century into the path of meteors.
Do all races prefer the numb slumber
of The End over Tomorrow's Cataclysm
of Red Mornings? The desert glows
like a pink planet. Backbones
of mountain ridges rise in brittle light,
as blue as brimstone. Charred necklaces
of cars rattle from Primm Valley
to Barstow. We fall silent,
mulling prophecies: Will jaundiced clouds
drip sulfuric mist? Whose dart pops
the black party balloon of time?
How will we look in our volcano baths,
sipping margaritas of moon ash,
our bodies Christmas boxes
of bones curled in ribbons of crispy skin?
The problem for descendants
of sun worshippers is no flint knife
carves a prayer chamber in your chest.
No fist of fire scoops your twitching heart
and spoons it into the hot wound
of heaven. Each orbit stifles a yawn
of belief in a bustling bazaar.
Rapture slips from the babble
of green parrots and fumbled baskets
of jipijapa leaves. Bloodlines thin
to a last chance for gas. But at this
late date something tells me
the 1-800-Who's-Your-Daddy? billboards

will remain as inscrutable as any
Dresden Codex. No doomsday will stop
the great-tailed grackles from flitting
like chatty reapers in silken cowls
through the honey locust trees
at the Family Plaza in Springville,
their nests capped in snowfall
two feet deep. Come Month of Zip!
Month of Uo! Chicken Licken kneels
before Kukulkan! Past Baker, California,
Home of the World's Tallest Thermometer,
a badger-faced woman in a blasted
Tioga camper, high priestess of the road,
speeds her grungy sons through
the creation myth of the day. She wears
the smile of the trickster, hub caps
flapping like rusty talaria. With my crew
asleep in back, I nudge the speedometer
to eighty, inches from her bumper,
seconds from painting a sacrificial stripe
of my family's blood on the highway.
A golden smear of bugs greases
our windshield, carcasses as sparse
as souls of slaves smashed at high speed,
the way we all hope to be killed.
Over the wheel I bow to her Kansas plates
and BMX bikes tangled like hieroglyphs
to read: *Assume the feeling of a wish fulfilled!*

II

SUBLIME DRIFT

A Presence

I return to Indiana County
to find small rabbits,
jumpy as the French Resistance,
have tunneled under
Studio C Hairstyling now
that the dope dealers
who used it as a front
don't stalk like sunburned refugees
past duct-taped windows anymore.
  A mosquito truce whirs
  where rhododendron violet peppers
  the red Bilco cellar door.

Summer is a presence that
wanders back to the sunken porch
of our last knowing.
Young canoe birches sprout skyward
and are toppled by beavers
in the time it takes you
to place a palm on chewed bark
as you cross charred leaf pulp
on a weedy riverside path.
  Late afternoon glare plunges
  its branding iron of rum
  in the copper current's aftermath.

Every return clears ground for
one that follows. Yellowthroats
plummet, and the earth gnaws
decades away. The eastern
black swallowtail, ecstatic
on drugs of daylight and air,
beats an erratic code for living
from wings of chimney-sweep soot,
a rhythm of glide and blunder.
  The subterranean heart races,
  bright as death in its warren,
  twitches like moon and thunder.

Poem That Will Never Be Turned into a Summer Blockbuster

Insert: American kestrels fluttering
like small kachinas of sky,
diving into roadside seas
of green wheat. They rise and hover,
crucified on air, flashy auburn flares
afloat in folklore sun. Man drives van.
Teenage daughters not speaking
to him. Reckless moods make him
surrender his Saturday to take
his oldest girl (riding shotgun)
and her friends to summer camp
in the hills of Swan Valley.
Background noise: gossip and boys,
mundane music of machines,
cackles and moans. Man eavesdropping.
Man feels silly, catching himself spying
on love as they swoop down
the paved spine of the raw landscape,
the serene and unsteady wheels
of turkey vultures as supple as ash,
miles above the gorge, awakening
in him the vision that the world
will end in bonfires of birds.
Zoom: the coarse yellow green
of bitterbrush, the monotone
of the service berry. The feeling
that they are escapees of some secret season.
Daughter plucks out a white earbud,
tells her friends she could marry
a veterinarian and live in a place like this.
Blank highway. Slopes of dead grass
studded with milky stones. Peaks overgrown
with scruffs of black pine. She inhales
and angles her sleepy face to say
(to nobody but maybe to him),
Summer's half gone. Man thinks, *I thought
the same thing when I held you seventeen years ago*

in a hospital thousands of miles
from here. Close up: claws clench,
talons drip the red of utterance.
Montage: the point of convergence,
the late departure, rocky gulches
running with rivers like brilliant ore.
Voice over: Long live long drives
in silence! Long live this hot-blooded
American sun! Traveler, drape me
in my mystical shawl of bronze feathers.
Release me into the swell of thermals.
Sharpen my sight. Streak the scent
of the kill on my tongue. Set my toes
at the cliff and spread the myth
of my scream over the lives of the young.

Sonnet: Breed

Harriman State Park, June 1999

Let me say that I envy the eared grebe.
Those orange flamenco sleeves, cloak dark as soot.
His heart bangs like a beast against his ribs.
Parades his passion with panache to boot.
I can't fan brash ear tufts and crest, as bold
as the rain god Tlaloc, shake lake droplets
like hot mercury on hammered gold,
can't mesmerize my lover, eyes blood-wet,
when the time comes to pass the genes along.
This cinderblock apartment is no nest.
We rendezvous in no caldera stream.
Still, lightweight and lovelocked, we'll sound our song
through gorges of blue stone, heedless of rest,
reborn with sun, wind, rock, sky, moss, air, dream.

Manent II

The winter's frail text stands.
Field and back road spread rutted lace.
  Serifed sparrows string pale reprimands
    from snow to snowless space.

    A flicker flees a naked limb.
Its underwings flash red-orange gleams
    from coals of smoldering hymns
      that warmed prehistoric dreams.

Trumpeter Swan/Beaver: 1/1/11

Here is my confession. When I said
I was leaving to run an errand
I meant walking to the cottonwood stand
behind the technical college to see
how many twisted trunks beavers had toppled
since last summer ground itself to sand.
I've done this for years.

Snow muted vacant lots. Ruts marred the place
where bulldozers gouged up wild poppies
we found. Cold spun breath to lace.
Light grazed my face, cooled on cars.
Ice burned. Fields and engineering offices
blazed with frigid gold in thin galleries.
The vivid always disappears.

A sound turned me. Half honk, half manifesto.
Seven swans, snowy flames from the river.
Big as A-10s, they skimmed treetops, so low
a man with a snow blower heard
them carve the air. Into pale sun they veered
at the velocity of white, through
the sky's cloudy gears.

Every confession is an errand.
I've tried to say this so you understand.
The urge to believe is the speech
of beavers perpetually unseen.
Every year, a ritual of arrivals, a futile reach
for the beauty of the fallen, the crash
that stills the thunder no one hears.

November Gale (Skaneateles, New York, 1993)

I. 2:45 p.m.

Six years back: you said we should take a walk
out on the lake's wind-roughened pier. Before
long, we braced ourselves there. Village boats knocked
at docks like fettered fowl. Behind inn's door,
your weekend clothes trailed, loose as vixen spoor.

II. 3:07 p.m.

We stood in the teeth of the wind. No words
came. The chill buffeting stole all our speech,
replaced by distant palettes of leaves, birds
flung in broad arcs of sky like peaked foam, each
tossed in the wind's fleet of gray, out of reach.

III. 3:08 p.m.

Then you turned. Your look proclaimed itself law:
to purge the sun's payload of faulted ore
that dropped through clouds to earth where you stood, or
to stall the glacier's six thousand-year thaw.

Death of a Fox

Harnham Road, Salisbury

To see a wild fox only twice in your life*
is a lament worthy of words. The summer
your dad died, crane flies blazed in the green air,

and I stepped from the trail
where a svelte male slunk across Glen Cove Road.
The sun tangled amber in his tangy coat

and paintbrush tail. I paused as if a queen
shed ermine robes and stepped nude
onto glossy mats of roadside myrtle.

Then I reversed tracks and walked back
with nothing to say. This morning, rain finer
than despair glosses the twisted remains

of that animal's English cousin where I round
a corner, thinking of other things—the body
mangled by savage automobile hounds,

teeth jutting like combs of angry ivory,
the slashed pelt sprinkled with a fine meal
of lilac blossoms, the glistening secret

of the hip joint as raw as steak,
tossed like a rough jewel for display on the foil
of wet tarmac. If there are answers

between you and me, one must be that each
morning of rain raises a ruined cathedral
of spired hours over love's fascinating wreckage

and the carcass of every day, by which
I can pass but from which I can't turn away.

*make that five times (as of September 2018)

A Small Thing

Loud geese revive the dark
   in August on Old Salt Road.
Dawn pours in grooves of bark
   a molten motherlode.

Acorn epics freefall
   from forest mezzanine.
Caps and capsules rattle
   parables of green.

Scarlet sumac candlesticks
   erect the many-in-one.
Ferrous doe and fawns make
   anecdotes of calm.

Keep Out. Private. Posted.
   Wilderness reversed.
Road Not Plowed or Sanded
   December to April First.

Raccoon shrinks in furrow clods,
   shines juvenile eyes.
Crow and seagull arcs explode
   like rafters of the sky.

A small thing is the greater.
   The storm, the swallow's swerve.
The swiftest particle of light,
   the sun's resounding curve.

Cycle

In a town ravenous for spring
the touch football games
break out in all quarters of Smith Park.
Near the orchestra gazebo
shoals of grit-flecked snow claim
most of the Ace Hardware day crew,
stiffarmed by their snakehipping

boss who does his best Red Grange
with bald spot, key ring, pocket protector.
Her liquid laughter arranged
in raw play, my daughter
escalades, step by step,
the Little Tikes jungle gym
the city splurged on, set in cedar chips.

At the bottom of the corkscrew slide
her feet splash down on a lump
of sloppy slush that at one time
shared the same sublime
drift as the B-22 iceberg now slumped
from the Thwaites Ice Tongue
into the Amundsen Sea tide,

roving like an emerald titan
the size of two Rhode Islands
over a watery planet some say
freezes and thaws simultaneously.
Near the seesaws, we dodge puddles.
I stoop for her stray shoe,
warming the wet world of my cells,

winter icing the spring sea
of my blood, while in Korea
a scientist beams in a news conference,
a flask of seawater in his fist,

harvested, he says, from trenches
off Greenland's coast, so deep it was
there at the birth of Christ.

Swimming in Buttermere

If I could choose how to go, it would be
like last May—on a rattletrap bus
called The Honister Rambler,

shuttled over picturesque fells
on narrow switchbacks and grumpy
transmission as one traveler among strange

but simple people. I would decode
the limpid banter of French backpackers
in the back seat, sneak glances

at the Cumbrian woman in navy
overcoat, her fossil fist clamped
on a tufted Corgi's leash, her arm babying

a jumble of clementines in a brown paper bag.
At a stile at the lake's north end,
I would decline the British Heritage ranger's

offer to join, explain that mine would be
a one-way trip. Having scaled
the vaulted face of Haystacks

to find the black rippled gem
of Wainwright's Innominate Tarn
in the wind-carved riddle of alpine crags,

I would descend in automatic strides,
bone-wearied and parched,
my feet finding my mind's path on the trail,

thrilled with a moment of nakedness
where I would don swim trunks in slashes
of sunny shadow in a sturdy camp

of conifers at water's edge. Pale pebbles
would press ascetic rapture
in the soles of my feet

before I would lower the jarred joints
of my soul into the aching clarity
of a thousand years of cataract runoff

and slip my head below the surface.
A cloud-haired German couple
balancing binoculars and box lunches

on knees, the last thing I would see.
The last thing I would hear:
the stop-your-heart scream

of an RAF fighter on maneuvers, the book
of sky ripped in half with nothing
but silence after, the bleating

of sheep sounding so much like laughter.

Buoyancy

These are the mornings soul could slip
from body like Archimedes

scampering nude through the streets of Syracuse,
robed in rosy steam from his bath.
In this wash of November light,

I could swap the midnight need
to know all for a fluid hour of floating,

spirit suspended on skin,
a white shower of cliff rose blossoms
lofted by young girls
in reckless moods
onto the swollen lens
of an untroubled pond on Lesbos.

These mornings the sodden sky
of All Souls' Day displays an empty proof
on which no diagram hangs.

Through the living room window
points of snow swarm
and swirl, plotting
the volume of our love and days
in the gray equation of dawn.

Silence laps the walls
in this empty house where I do the math

that finds us and the stranded trucker
in oil-smudged hooded sweatshirt
who blows heat into his hands
and tries to jumpstart his orange Peterbilt rig
in the parking lot

leaving this impure drop
of a world lighter for our absence—

skittish water skippers scattering
across pond ripples, milkweed fluff
blown from a blinding stream in summer,

the vapor exhaled in our final Eureka.

Tree as Lens

for R. F.

A willow brings morning in tune
inside an hour, trapping points of dew,
itself a drop of green blue.

A still-life photo at noon.
Part filter and formula the veins hold,
synthesizing all stray gold.

Seven o'clock goes orange too soon,
when it drops a red mosquito load,
its most variable mode.

In the Harriet Tubman Home

With twenty-first century aplomb
and baby girl in arms, I approach
a White model sewing machine
that glows like a worn altar
and gaze out a window through
the loose bunting of pale green sun.
Across ungroomed grounds
chain gangs of summer shuffle
through glad eruptions of tiger lilies.
Savaged orange safety mesh
and steel poles angled like black bones
cordon off the archeological dig
where Syracuse University,
our guide Christine says, is scavenging
for God knows what.

A blond boy in our group swings
his forearm cast like a ragged messenger
bearing the gift of heaviness.
Rank-and-file sinners,
we board the pale blue shuttle bus
to our final comeuppance
as the driver commiserates
with the boy's scruffy dad
over the dangers of skateboards
then describes the blackout fits
a teenage Harriet entered
when she said the voice of God
told her where and when to go.

On the way to the Seward Mansion,
the hoarse intercom asks
if there are any questions.
Can you have a memory of something
you never experienced?
Why else the chiseled conviction
that my child and I worshipped

in the solid pews of the A. M. E. Zion Church
and wandered the misty hummocks
of Fort Hill? From the muddy shell
of a giant turtle did we watch
Sky Woman plummet and give birth
to twin sons, Sapling and Flint?
When will we harbor our fugitive woes
and from the museums of our homes summon
those who come to hear what God knows?

Prostitute: San Francisco

The back seat of the grimy taxi
my mother herded me into
when I was twelve, when remembered,
can still summon the smell
of a pack of chainsmoking hacks
choking on the same stale jokes.
Don't look can mean look
at what you didn't see in the first place.
The woman's brash cocktail dress,
red velour, looked like someone lashed
a tacky theater curtain
around the burlesque act of her body.
Ruin rouged her face, a harried
portrait of a Punchinello
smeared by the hand of an angry child.
Sidewalk sloped under her heels
of glossy black magic, making one leg
longer than the other, so now
I see her as a sex compass, carving
ritual circles into faded lives,
or one of those folklore mountain goats
from Italy or the Swiss Alps,
caught only when hounded
to level ground where, hapless,
they scamper around, hunted where
anything virgin can no longer astound.
If we say *Don't love* will we love
what we haven't seen? To my younger
self I can still say, and sometimes do:
You don't need to sell yourself
for streets of surrender. In the fanfaronade
of night traffic, the baroque flames
blooming from hissing grills
in Japanese restaurants, you can send
the golden earthquake drumming
beneath buildings of blind fog,
through the slums of slack heartbeats,

and from back seats and sullen harbors
arrive in the city of lights to find
your innocent life faithfully waiting.

Short Discourse on Species

Five days after the vicious frost of All Souls' Day I shed my college
      sweatshirt in fifty degrees of Saturday, and I am surprised,
      digging in the garden while somewhere off Anger Island in the
      Great Bear Rain Forest scruffy biologists and Heiltsuk guides
      harvest gray wolf scat in vials to find traces of steelhead, Sitka
      black-tailed deer, and tidbits of black bear.

And I am planted in the paradox of bear as both destroyer and hors
      d'oeuvre, the warm spade of sun sinking hunger in my vitals as
      I tear into the slurry of mud with the savage relish of a carnivore.
      I yank pale nets of Chinese parsley and blunt carrot shards from
      sockets of sloppy earth. The bloodless tendons of bean vines I ply
      from a jerry-rigged trellis of plumber's pipe and yellow twine.
      Aborted tomatoes clack like river rocks, hardened to the color of
      smoky quartz.

The cycle of decay and renewal spares nothing. All survival is consigned
      to a dirty five-gallon bucket, carted off as waste and the food of
      life that I am.

And here I am, heart roaring with a final charge, swinging my shovel
      like the Lord's besom of destruction, shattering clods and frail
      spindles of jewel mix nasturtiums. I bare fangs like the alpha
      male guarding a half-chewed carcass when my daughters stray
      near the mess in white sneakers and clean pink pants. Who—
      shaggy boar or rogue scientist in bullet kayak—divines the truth
      of this life-in-death motif? Of autumn disguised for a day in
      summer's speckled hide? The how and why of daughters
      born to die? Hear the nitrogen from dead chum salmon swell
      pine needles on the evergreen top. It is the sound of knowing we
      are the reaper and the crop.

Hidden Motion

Someone explain why through summer sun
that clatters on this suburban culdesac
like heaps of brass artifacts

Galileo's rider gallops on horseback,
arm extended to drop a cannonball
earthward, proving to skeptic papists all

that we and the lapsed world free fall
in tandem, skydive through cloudy chaos
and spindly constellation so most

of our flight stays as unseen as ghosts.
All day this ravenous desert wind
throttles panes and tangles telephone lines,

snapping four-inch thick aspen on Main,
making the crab tree we planted jones
like a sixteenth-century lunatic in chains.

Someone explain why I remain
at the kitchen window for an age,
gaunt homebound astronomer who won't budge

until he claims proof that in this mirage
of days we move forward, swooped
into the saddle, cantering off, clip-clop,

from the yard still ragged with uncropped
weeds, down the mossy cobbled design
of time's telescoping corridor where we can

wait to witness the heresy of light undone.

Pennsylvania Pantoum

the low firebrand sun a smeared medallion
gunmetal vapors that blunt silo domes
deer carcass angles death's brown figurine
screech and jeer blue jay cries ancient murder

gunmetal vapors that blunt silo domes
skunk buggy caravan sheer coal train lisp
screech and jeer blue jay cries ancient murder
my anger your waiting the spaces between

skunk buggy caravan sheer coal train lisp
short-circuit yellow marquee that says Andy's
my anger your waiting the spaces between
firefly tracers ricochet off windshield

short-circuit yellow marquee that says Andy's
ghost cattle torque forces hinges of bone
firefly tracers ricochet off windshield
stampede of stillness on Kintersburg Bridge

ghost cattle torque forces hinges of bone
your spacious anger my waiting between
stampede of stillness on Kintersburg Bridge
sumac tiers tangle clots of cardinal flight

your spacious anger my waiting between
the clatter of the dead on the Knox & Kane
sumac tiers tangle clots of cardinal flight
daybreak ignites bronze fusillade of blue

the clatter of the dead on the Knox & Kane
deer carcass angles death's brown figurine
daybreak ignites bronze fusillade of blue
the sun a medallion smeared firebrand low

The Cadenza

The composed snows of April second
drape the scrubby hills east
of Willow Creek in ten new blues.

Past the Riverside Drive exit
a pewter El Dorado with California plates
passes us on our highway cruise

to my childhood home.
Mozart's piano concerto
in E flat major sweetens the car radio.
The host in butterscotch tones

announces the evening's tribute
to the cadenza, which my wife tells
me is a variation on a theme
where the piece seems

about to end but then goes on.
We are two adults
and three young girls traveling

past the town of Firth
and a semi truck trailer improvised
into a billboard for Vollmer Well Drilling.

Time transposes us as we ride
toward and away from my eighteenth summer
when my wife and daughters
were no more material

than the bright stains of sun
that soaked shaggy clumps
of dry lace vines over the doorway
to the wooden garden shed

I stained on that endless Saturday
in my Bandits practice jersey and denim shorts,
midway along this debut flight

toward the diminishing point where
things seem about to end but then go on.

At Once People at the End of Their Lives

come from common spaces to move around
the fountains and the flowers of Hyde Park.
They appear early, soundless, as if shod
in slippers of sleepwalkers. They embark
then pause, each breath the birth of a small god.
Thoughts enter them like planets run aground.

It is the pools of their eyes the time zones
cloud. They bring skies of rouge from Arkansas,
toy moons from Seoul. Statues open trench coats
and out shuffle the listless nudes. Hurrah
for the mumbled chant, the clearing of throats,
for the slower machinery of bones.

Watch the lavender of young orchids drain
from their cardigans. Trace the wet brushstrokes
of thinning blood. On some subsonic stair
the threadbare amens and the feeble jokes
ascend only to spiral in the air,
leaving no stain or the sound of a stain.

In bright rosebush labyrinths, they converge,
look up, blink, turn, and reverse the dazed prowl.
Unfinished: the cosmic wheel of their dance.
The starved grass crawls. Archways blacken. A surge
of sun shatters on patchwork waterfowl
and enters the drowsy eye like a lance.

Still River

For the sake of motion, leave your lover
in a third story hotel room
on Shoup Avenue in November.
Trade the vagrant space of your body
for an energetic pace through
a sallow cone of streetlamp haze.
Adopt as your spiritual twin
the wolfman drifter in grungy
Cubs jacket who emerges from
a Celica to rob a curbside ATM.
In the savings and loan's eighteen degrees,
translate a lust for permanence
into the morning edition ejected
from a Post Register truck. Outside
Vino Rosso, reserve a table for
death's banquet of burgundy and rattan.
Exhale transience opposite the opera house.
Channel showstopper applause for
the burlesque pony act evicted
from the Oddfellows Hall a century
before Saving Center taped butcher paper
ads for rock bottom canned ham.
Circumvent east and west banks—
where circuits of black ice and cattails
stall galleries of mallards on
seamless water and hotels bristle
an archeology of lost nights. Seize
new means to deny the temporary earth.
Try memory. The Stellar's jay that
strafed your office window with
the propaganda of August, neon blue
feathers nettled in a Russian olive's
green-silver papyri. Or Amherst nuns.
The pair that glided magpie devotion
from St. Brigid's to pass pins of May gold
to homeless men amid the lisp of traffic
and espresso cafés. And a Wyoming spring.

Your car parked at a turnout
on Pacific Creek. A quartet of otters
savaged quicksilver trout. The rosy flesh
of valley sod ruptured under
April's anxious claws. Then a surge of swan
wingbeats inscribed a tetralogy
of white sky across the days before
you returned to your lover, the unfinished
axiom of the world in your hands,
partly forged in stillness, part still river.

III

RARE MEASURE

The Poem of the Future

will be a jumpsuit of perpetual energy,
a popsicle of sadness.
The humming hangar where a snarl
of test tubes and electrodes
gets clipped to your tongue, fingers, retinas,
eardrums, and nostrils. You will suck
liquefied poem of the future
through mucus-tipped antennae
and digest it for seven years
before dropping the ovoid gold seeds
in gray loam. The poem of the future
will run on the afflatus
of the dung beetle. It will coo
and moo. It will come equipped
with mood-controlled, octo-directional,
zinc-infused thrusters. With a third
penis. With a hooked foreclaw
as sharp and gnarled and yellow
as a warlock's toenail, perfect
for digging escape tunnels, goring rivals,
and scooping out their greasy
purple guts. The Ministry of Editorial Taste
will streamline and mass produce
the poem of the future. To use:
1) tear open the silver packet
and 2) squeeze the red protein-enriched
paste on your soul. Embracing
the poem of the future will require
the absolute surrender of the will.
The poem of the future will be so far
ahead of anything anyone
has thought of, when in anti-gravity
body pod you power up your coil
of holographic cantatas in Central Park—
even at your work's debut—people will
dismiss you as a beatnik prophet
with a doomsday sign as they throng

the colorful jumble of rented kebab wagons
and ice cream vans like asylum seekers,
and only one or two will glance
at what you have brought the world,
and even those few, so addled with the stress
of life, will forget what they saw
before they arrive home.

To People Who Talk to Themselves in Cars

Very often people don't listen to you when you speak to them
It's only when you talk to yourself that they prick up their ears
                                    —John Ashbery

Why does your face slump
like a mountainside in the slanted rain
of shame at this busy stoplight?
Because my sidelong glance
yanks the plug from your sexy soliloquy
to a Saturday of imaginary suitors
who conga down a catwalk
in lemon bow ties and shimmery blue boxers
of borrowed desire? The mouth,
blind bullet, explodes through
the cracked windshield of the soul.
So why crestfallen, as if snitching
snickerdoodles from my sister's lunchbox?
Fellow psychobabbler, trumpet your disease.
What the hell? What the brain?
What the problem? What the pain?
Sometimes spitting seeds of secrets
in the soundproof studio
of your stalled Chevy Nova is all you can do.
The solution: Make verb vector
and susurrus sonic boom. Murderer munching
mnemonics, lawyer lisping a libretto
of lies—you are not broken.
Think of *Homo erectus* waylaid in crowds
at The Olduvai Gorge, airing his
laundry list of lost loves. Ask the Shanghai
taxi driver chewing his Taoist cud
at rush hour if with the end of movement
words begin. On your Day of Pent-up-cost,
speak in tangents. Filibuster
in the senate of sin. No one mumbles voodoo
on the boss without a supporting cast
of lousy ventriloquists. We are all

the American Housewife in mousy housecoat
at the pharmacy window, addendums
to St. Augustine leaking from our faces.
We are, on Planet Gridlock, one race
playing a big blues gig on air harmonica,
and the universal translation is
Life sucks and traffic is bad. So let the spigot
of the subconscious roar full bore.
Shower us in syllables of sybilline sibilance.
Red lights turn green. Murmured prayers
free the turning lane. The myopic Manchurian
on opium, the senile ex-producer
humming Gary Numan lyrics, they make way
for the one who waits to receive
your Freudian French kiss, the one who will
drive and listen as long as you can ramble.

Hymn for the Control Freak

Lord, scope the skulls of rebels
and tell me how they lie to themselves.
The Wat Tylers and Boxers
of Shangdong, the Angolas and States
of Jefferson stocked with squatters
who occupy and mutineers who march.
Open their eyes to the tyranny
of nonconformity. Tune the ears
of the world to freedom singing
in its cage, "Oh, Human Will,
Lock without Key." Add my proverb
to yours: "No porch swings
without breezes" (Gospel of Me 1:1).
The ice cream man needs this
the most, the gummy-eyed guy
in ragged pumpkin T-shirt who prowls
in his wheezy wagon down our street
from Memorial Day to the equinox.
His mother, wheelchair-bound,
rides in back with the fudgesicles
like Norman Bates mimicking
Whistler's mother in repose,
fuzzy red quilt over her knees.
Speakers blast "God Rest Ye Merry
Gentleman" through the neighborhood
all July, and my six-year old son
dashes in to bash his ceramic
piggybank to dust then races outside
with a buck in change to worship
curbside for a frozen treat
he could claim elsewhere for a dime.
He waits, hands raised, a cultist
sans culottes, stained copper
dripping from his clutches, head cocked
for the sultry tune of the Pied Piper
of the Rainbow Rocket Pop.
Dusk purples the street corner

where he searches the fine liberation
of this lemon-lime summer,
the anarchy of his blood and August air
flavored with the trill of goldfinches
in a brittle gallery of sunflowers,
the chirps sounding like small shears.
Make my son come in. Make him
stop waiting for delight that never appears.

In All the Novels

I've written in my head
cars barrel down icy highways
on bald tires. Each rescued part
comes from another car
so people race toward trouble
in the colorful wrecks
of other people's mistakes.
Much is mismatched and patched together.
Diners always fold. An ex-marine
with a mustache and shaggy brown hair
stands below a twisted fire escape
in his blue and gold Arlington Honkers
varsity jacket and gazes
at an arched window that burns
like a portrait of yellow
in a dark office building
after midnight. The heroine clutches
a black and white dance hall photo
of her grandmother and weeps.
Her brass suitcase latch breaks
and all the fan letters
she wrote to herself scatter
in the hot Nebraska windstorm.
Comedy douses sadness the way
the moon melts into winter mountains.
A bozo billionaire and religious cult
in strawberry togas provide the escape.
An abandoned barn of field mice
and exhumed boot, the brooding interludes.
For thirty years I add and delete
the passage in which I grow older,
a minor character goading
the author's streamlined dreams.
In this scene I drive my last two children
down a straight highway, November
a still life of ferocious white, as colorless
as prose. I am painting over

the salvage jobs of love. Breath makes
windows opaque. Snow erases
the black seams of railroad tracks,
our silence like the pleasure
of tension mounting. So many swans
cover a lake, we stop counting.

On All the Park Benches

where I sit some deceased nobody
makes resting a forced memorial.
You should be able to relax
without mounted plaques
making you slouch in the ghosts
of strangers like a vagrant
trying on a dumpster of used bathrobes.
Who cares about the Beth Williamses
and green gazebos in Everett,
Washington, "Because She Loved This Place";
The Shane and Sharon Vandygriffs
on concrete contours at a South Dakota
rest stop, "Remembered Fondly";
the Jeremiah Renfrew-Shakars
bolted to polished salmon sandstone
in a Henderson suburb, "Never Gone,
Never Forgotten"? Who can savor
reverie with the dead crowding
our down time, waving scanty résumés
like third graders believing
the store-bought valentines
in their hands, always hijacking
the social elevator to the penthouse
with the glass rotunda? This is my memo
to the parks office: I shall not
reincarnate as a picnic shelter
where stepmothers in orange sweat pants
can chow cheeseburgers and chase
pedophiles with reptile eyes
from their skeletal second chances.
No matter who comes to you
with fat donation envelopes, no matter
the sentimental slogans or hand-made
brass designs, strew my ashes
in the water supply so when people
spread gaudy patchwork quilts
and unpack ham sandwiches in the sun

like penitents sacrificing to the gods
of leisure, I'll send them screaming
from the sudden shower of the sprinklers
on the one memorable day
I gave them comfort in my nameless rain.

I Will Never

be one of those guys
who wears a T-shirt in the pool.
Mistakes should stay
as naked as an unfrosted cake.
When my body bloats
like The Blob's wet dream,
have the nearest crane operator
dump me in the deep end
as bare as the day
I spoke my first syllables of pain.
I will never say, "Well, I never!"
Never go undercover
or wave banners for lies.
Never carouse. Never arrive.
From bleachers I'll never badmouth
someone's fifth-grade girl
on the basketball court.
Never vacation in Mexico
the way my brother does,
sending photos of my nephew
swimming with dolphins
under a sky blue enough to blind
the sun while I drive my used car
around this northwestern town,
the gray snow and grainy light
a guarantee for six months,
the constant sky a carbon slate,
the storefronts a kingdom of shadows.
Never will I favor despair,
breed retrievers, or savor a stare
like the one I receive
from a shivering coffee-eyed girl
on Christmas Eve, her wet ponytail
a squiggle of ink, her dream
to splash for a steamy hour
with her bashful dad and five sisters
in this roadside motel.

Each stout brunette girl
has stepped out of her mother
like the Matryoshka of the Month,
to the ear the endless echo
of a giggle, to the eye
the evolutionary stages of the soul.
The mother reclines
on an aquamarine deck chair,
the baby wedged between
her thighs like the young goddess
carved on the prow of a ship.
Her quick needles knit
an afghan of fuzzy blue yarn—
something I could never do—
as if to say, *Whatever happens*
I will never let my hands leave this miracle.

I Realized Today

at this guy's funeral that my death
will not be a musical event.
Six former students
of the guy who died performed
his original compositions
with graceful glancing strokes
across silvery xylophones
and glossy marimbas and vibes
arranged like aircraft carriers
for angelic bombers
or sonic steppingstones ascending
from the sunburst floral sprays
at the front of the crowded church
to the soundproof studio
of the next world.
The paunchy former students
were packed into wrinkled suits
of powder blue linen
with retro stovepipe trousers
and highwater cuffs in the style
of Teddy Boys and Mods,
as if bodies were botched etudes
or notes they once reached.
Imagine flubbing the maestro's scores
as his critical soul hovered
in a reserved pew, fingers interlocked,
ear cocked for slack tempo,
his metronome of bones
clocking off perfection,
his cork-handled baton slashing down
its vicious ivory to sting
your bloodless knuckles
then passing through *pianissimo*
like the hiss of condolences.
To those who will conduct:
Gear my eulogy to ungifted silence.
I want one bouquet of left feet and tin ears.

Awkward dead space, my eulogy.
My eulogy: a benefit mime concert
for volunteer dolphin trainers
with cancer, generations
after which students of my eulogy
and students of their students
in an assembly of accidents
will reprise variations on joy
and grief, improvising staccato coughs
and standard sighs of rare measure,
ringing like blood in the ears
of a muted room of offbeat hearts.

American Anthem

Outside Biaggi's, teens in creamy gowns
and tuxes pass panhandlers in the blind parade.
Dusk stains sidewalks pink. Busses lurch.
Stretched limos promenade. A glum vet,
slim as a blade of candlelight, sinks bills
in his sneaker, claws a scrawny ankle.
At the traffic light, Elvis Costello's scuzzy double
begs means to perch bedside for a dying aunt
in Canada. Should we wonder that
the world is a street corner? Everywhere
you wait, the desire of the day
scrawls a menu of myths on a cardboard sign.
Plush voices crack, ordering a fantasy,
and the man pours the wine. This is
your country. Land of the Guarded Stare.
Hunger scuffs the floor in a dim gymnasium
of sappy ballads and snags the last
slow dance in a room of overturned chairs.
In the same half hour, you can meet two women,
both in their eighties, one asking about
the neighbor boy's suicide, the other
with a snapshot on her avocado fridge—
her only son, dead for all she knows.
Evenings, shove your toes in combat boots,
don a grungy skirt and loose lemon blouse,
slouch against a streetlight, boyfriend in your lap,
while he cadges smokes from Jazz fans.
You can watch mobs of starlings jab rinds
of sunlight in the gutter, wear on your
exposed breast a corsage of grime.
Your standing reservation can be the newest way
to seem, to find a place to sit and never
get over the day someone handed you a dream.

Shame and Guilt

Rise before dawn to jog the parking lot around the Liberty Sleep Inn, the traffic on the wet highway a slow rip in the curtain of the universe, the air a soupy haze. With the one good eye of a man who has abandoned memory, believe in colored lights bleeding from the bleary world. Count chain smokers clustering around the exits like shoddy supplicants at The Neon Temple of the Butane Flame. Their translucent flesh glows like onionskin pages. The rumpled surfing T-shirts and khaki shorts they have slept in match the humble robes of pilgrims. When they glance up then cast down their eyes, cradling cursed wombs, wonder if you are the founder of a new American religion. The one that fuses all doctrines and summons the final awakening. No commandments, no tomes, no sadness. Only the wise red sun smiling in the eyes of those who embrace The Three Affirmations:

> *In you beats the Blood of Revolution!*
> *In you roars the Breath of Reformation!*
> *In you blazes the Golden Sunrise of Eternal Rebirth!*

A beer-bellied truck driver in green golf shirt and pure white sneakers limps from the strip mall and, witnessing your ascension from the cigarette butt he flicks under your shoe, becomes a wandering sage. His good-will caravan rambles to remote hideaways so every outcast who sees the grinning black woman, redhead, Hispanic man, bald spectacled man with a gray mustache, and blond mother on the side of his HyVee Foods truck knows the ancient tribes cleansed the movement of racism, sexism, ageism, heightism, hairism, and ismism. No remorse, only the sacred blossom of the open throat. No blame, only cicadas in horsetail grass, drumming the burden of a Missouri summer from their backs, sawing brittle tunes on camp fiddles. For a totem, a jackrabbit darting from shrubs like the frightened heart seeking sanctuary. For a marvel, a mystical figure materializing in the shape of a disgruntled city worker on the overpass at the height of the commute. With a voice of warning he proclaims that he descends from an alien race that watched earth for eons but now lives among the blind and proud. He pleads for the chosen ones to welcome the bullet of belief that stills the heart. The cause joins you, he calls, to the vast shooting gallery of martyrs, the cars and trucks roaring like a relentless urge into the amplified soul of Kansas City. If you don't resist, he whispers over the guardrail, taking aim. If you keep moving and don't stop to think you may never have to feel again.

The Fool

All it takes is a late March sky on Saturday morning, clouds as rare as ideas cycling above the weedy black soil that I slash and overturn with a garden spade in my backyard, and I'm remembering Willis Pitkin in his reading glasses, purple turtleneck, and jeans—how he paused at the blackboard midstream in his transformational-generative grammar lecture in the cellar of the Ray B. West Building to say that every institution needs a Shakespearean

fool. Someone who could make jokes about whatever he wanted whenever he wanted

without fear of reprisal. A fertile hypothesis. But you might question the humor in some settings. Imagine this fool in Dallas on a grassy knoll, in tri-pronged bell-tipped hat, a miniature version of his head on a stick, two long stockings of Christmas red and green and a jaunty gold codpiece, tenderizing the crowd with the punch line from

the *how many conspirators does it take to change a president?* joke in the frantic wake of the Kennedy motorcade. Perhaps you see him in vaudeville straw hat and candystripe jacket as he softshoes in from stage left to "Swanee River" through passion fruit trees and lush hedges, just before Satan gives Eve the apple. Sweating in the footlights, he slips a three-by-five notecard into Adam's hand and prompts him with the penciled line, "Take my wife, please!"

Or maybe he donned trench coat and Groucho Marx nose and glasses before tapping Walter Ulbricht on the shoulder and quipped sardonically that "something there is that doesn't love a wall and wants it down." Perhaps we can see him disguised as a janitor on MIT's ivy-espaliered campus in 1955, sneaking a whoopee cushion under Noam Chomsky as the old anarchist sits down, forever disrupting revolutionary visions of the hook-and-eye

wonder of English grammar, hundreds of verb and noun phrases shattering on the concrete floor like cheap cafeteria plates. Exactly what you see depends on you. But I know I could have used him after school in

1983 behind PDQ Fried Chicken 'n' Taters, surrounded by toppled Coke billboards and U-haul trailers, when Delfin Ordaz and some kid with braces and a sleazy brushstroke mustache screeched up in a white GMC pickup and

asked if I was being a smart ass. I could have used him at that moment
        with a rubber chicken or coconut cream pie in their faces while
        I bolted for home. Even on this jubilant March weekend as I
        hack spadefuls of sodden, tar-colored earth while half a world
        away satellite-guided bombs rain the flame-tailed tulips of black
        spring on Baghdad like one bad idea after another, I take comfort
        in knowing he's probably in Basra where

        renegade guerillas hanged an Iraqi woman with a surrender flag
from a streetlight. There he hands out Xeroxed fliers on which people read
the real reason why the chicken crossed
the road. I'm sure he kneels near a marine in the furor of the food riots in
Umm Qasr, loosens
a tourniquet, elevates a plasma bottle for an IV, and whispers in the fallen
man's ear, inches from where Kalashnikov rounds punched dimples in his
Kevlar helmet, a word

of hope in a hackneyed line about a priest, rabbi, and imam walking into
a bar together.

Taking Goethe to the Eastern Idaho State Fair

Would the Father of German Romanticism
be caught more dead than he is
in this twilight of the goons?
From four states every parolee
in embroidered boots and eye shadow
the color of new bruises has invaded
Bonneville County like a bad case
of bluetongue. From space this rendezvous
must redden the shaved rump
of the planet. Puffs of powdered sugar
rise from the electrified sea
of neon wheels, and a haze of cooking oil
glazes these September stars.
"Der Prokurator" in the white paperback
in my shoulder bag might have answers,
but I've paid three bucks to park
on warped plywood in someone's yard
and walked off without getting
the girl's name. Stoic statesman
and patriot, I've staked a small republic
at the sprained gates of the kiddie pirate ride
so my children can whirl in laughing
circles for the hundredth time.
Who is lonelier? The artist or man
who is sad at the heart of the carnival?
This apprenticeship of young sorrows
I mull next to a scraggly dad,
half trapped in his nicotine stare.
His weedy hair sprouts from a crumpled cap.
His spectacled daughter peels
a Band-Aid from her nose,
her funhouse smile as wide as
this day of court-ordered custody.
Do they not see the immorality
of the fried Twinkie? The bold tragedy
of aquamarine dreadlocks? Ear gauges
large enough to usher in a new age?

We believe we overlook tattooed cleavage,
that half the rides bear signs saying
"Michael Jackson's Neverland Ranch."
Ah, to be beloved and sold secondhand!
To know you can no more lose
your place among used amusements
than you can escape your fabled race.
To this we are resigned at closing time,
tempted and delivered, the way
we arrived, descendants of
the frozen strawberry lemonade sun.
Here, a Dixie cup of oats for Tater,
the miniature foal born yesterday.
Now an extra dollar tickled
from our pockets to see the pig
bigger than Napoleonic pride.
Smashed popcorn bags and strawed manure
underfoot, in our clanging hearts
the *Sturm und Drang* of another summer
gone, another hour spent praying
for a shady bench far from
beer garden and cowboy karaoke tent.
On our hypnotist lips, the tacky
purple sugar of a story, a merchant,
a former bachelor from a seaport
on the Italian coast, the clumps
of fig-sized gems he bestows
on his young wife's breast, the questions
when he must leave on a long voyage.
Will she be faithful? Will she seduce
the handsome lawyer who passes
her window bay? Will any of us end
up happy? Will anyone remember this day?

IV

FIRST ECHO

Ernest Hemingway Boxes Ezra Pound: A Primer

The incubus of incunabula
leads with his chin. Ample Pamplona!
The amplitude of your alps

I relish in the austerities of August,
the flushed arrivistes in your eyes.
Breed the fever of the new brood,

my plush chums. Gallant gallivanting Gallicans!
Who reproves Prometheus rains
poundings of punchdrunk prose.

Who renews ruin, palooka or panjandrum,
raises in the rival face lush blood
as purple as Paris in June.

This year spirals down Mussolini's ear canal.
This year they jail matadors for debt.
This year, stick and move on taut tiptoes,

dodging the dance, these rueful afternoons,
colloquy of left hooks and sweaty grins.
How will you reclaim the scripta continua

of the times? Return, refugee.
The war is healing scars on trees.
Return to where the enemy slug spun

the changed language of your axis.
Always will the red of your ragged knees
match the painted villas, each a vacant heart.

Always the scandent clouds of summer,
fleeting and finer than Swiss napery,
buoy the true timbre

of a good review. So many toros
under the mazarine wound of the moon.
So many rivers overgrown in green interludes.

Soccer Dads

drawl like stock sidekicks
in penny dreadfuls. They hector and crow.
Gladhanding soccer dads glower
when lowballed, in glancing snowfall
swoon when the old sadnesses prowl
through them like trawlers
on jeweled seas of spectral red lights.
Their soundtrack solos on the bassoon.
Q: When exactly did soccer dads
explode the mold for bowlegged buffoons?
A: When the first soccer dad,
known only as Rec Primus,
was exhumed from a bog in Provence,
his stony black bones
in the slackened and sloped pose
of a loner prone to luxuriate
in grandstands like a suntanned sultan
soaking in a mineral pool
of miracle moods. In fruitless collusion
with better news, the soccer dad—
no slugabed, no slouch—in wolfman crouch
measures the golden mouth
of hope under the lowliest moon.
Raffish, often retrograde, he strolls forth
with silver-tipped retorts
as smartly as when the rosters
of rollercoasting dead take sides.
His swallow-winged curses swirl
like paternosters over drooping upstarts
too downtrodden to rise. He is born
and becomes an artifact before our eyes.

The Persian Legends

    say the slaves of Tyre in a revolt slew every free citizen and grabbed
the wheels of government on their glittering Oz in the sea as the last smear
of sun slid from the blue blade of the horizon and the Mediterranean
moaned and shed its robes of purple gold like a shadow sinking from the
walls of a public brothel. One rebel, taking pity, hid his master's son in
a closet. That boy, Strato, later became king on the festival day the city
declared the first one to spy sunrise would claim the throne. Rather than
strain east with the rabble he spun west and cried out when the molten blaze
of morning struck the tallest buildings. From Strato came "stratosphere"
and "Stratocaster"—not true, I know, but it sounds like something we
should believe. In truth, you can't prove the Persian legends didn't give us
the lonely jobs of local weathermen or the mythic reverberations of Buddy
Holly and Yngwie Malmsteen. These aren't the Persian legends, anyway,
but the annals of Justin, who sounds less like the Roman epitomator of
Thorgus, and more like the freckled redheaded kid from the apartments
next door, whose parents must be gypsies because whenever you glance up,
he's teleported from Planet Howdy Doody in his cruddy pizza-stained
T-shirt and shimmery green track pants to ask if you're moving. And when
you stare through sunglasses without answering like an idol from the
underworld, his bubble-gum lips bend a smile rimmed with grime, and
he sidles on filthy ape feet into your garage for the daily ritual of smashing
your tools and children's toys across the altar of his historical rage. And
the Persian legends seem as distant as the moon on the Aegean Sea, white
blossoms dripping sensuous mockery inches from your fingers. Then
poplars sway, your tyrant bones mellow to estuaries of September light,
and you are a golden god in the unpainted chair behind your house, eyes
shut in prayer to the choral chant of your blood, murmuring to a gathering
of scribes about how your mother, the night she conceived you, dreamed
she was coiled in a snake with eyes of smoky twilight, and two eagles
perched on your father's palace, one for the foe you would vanquish, the
other for the thousands of times the stories would change
    on pilgrimages to your tomb.

Allen Iverson

went to prison two months
before I was married.
Known as The Answer,
he questioned his time
in Detroit and Memphis,
called his return to Philadelphia
a gift from God. I have
known some to call God
and marriage a prison.
I have found one month
a question and another
an answer. Anything can be
your God if you return
what you have known
to be a gift. Anything can marry
question and answer
in time. So many prisons
of knowing have returned me
to months before
when I found something
calling me to question.
When he suffered,
Allen Iverson asked
his grandmother, *Why is God
doing this to me?* She answered:
Never question God.

Though

this sudden maze of April rain dashes
every square of sidewalk with
the crazed verve of a mad impressionist,
the cloudburst crashing, glazing gray pavement

as though born to emblazon
the ground with slashes of fresh chaos,
swerving and smashing
a splashed camouflage on porches and curbs

as though flicked from the fibers
of some tormented brush—
though I watch from where I'm trapped
behind glass—the drops fly as dew shaken

from lilies tossed and crushed
under the hooves of the hero's grazing mare,
as whole notes blown from the bell
of primal spring, now that I consider desire

at the window, feeling it hard to want
any other thing than to know
that rains pass, and the glory astonishes
in the passing when I step out on our street

after the sun-sparked droplets have stopped
rolling down invisible strings, clashing
in a rhapsody of gutters where I can hold
my baby girl to the light as a symbol

of desire and see the silken hair in the curve
of her neck blaze as though part of an endless fire.

All Words

I guess I realized it   was   all words

        seven months into
         my job as assistant copywriter

for

   The Haworth Press, Inc., Binghamton, NY (No. 16 Alice Street,

     a somber chocolate creme and beige
     cinder-

   block warehouse down by the Susquehanna River and railroad bridges,

[up Robinson Street the state psychiatric
         hospital crouched like
       a smoky castle in a deep green cumulus of trees]

And it was June, I believe—
           the day was a smudged symphony   of silver

                   smog, yellow trumpeting

         butter-flies, and cheeseburger wrappers
flung about the street like translucent bandages for grease wounds.

Cracked
sidewalks raised ragged flags

   of crabgrass
        near the company dumpsters. (The car crushers   were
         hammering away

two streets
     over @ Ben Weitzman & Sons [the scrap metal merchants])

all words: I

        realized.

because I'd just finished writing   a headline.

For Sister Bridget Claire McKeever's (PhD):
        Hidden Addictions: Prescription Drug Dependency
    in the
Elderly.

NOW, THIS EASY-TO-UNDERSTAND CUTTING-EDGE PUBLICATION WILL HELP YOU AND THOSE NEAR AND DEAR TO YOU AID THE ELDERLY IN YOUR LIFE IN BREAKING THE CRIPPLING STRANGLEHOLD OF PRESCRIPTION DRUG ADDICTION!

    And

        I guess

        it   was

        the exclamation point

that did   it

        ping!

    Just

swinging

        out

        there.

like some leaky party balloon or donkey-less tail,

paralyzed phallus, bent propeller,
some obscene

swizzle stick stabbed in a cork

(and *I'd* typed it),

or a hazel-green damselfly,

liberal aeronaut, careening

around your
porchlight on a humid evening

after a barbeque with people you've pretended to be friends with for years.   It was
like

my red-haired, blue-eyed daughter
tugging at the string of those cheapo $1.99 kites

I always buy her—

wanting both the flight of release

and craving
control,

In the same moment, without spending   any   thing.

But I knew it was:
instantly, there, creaking in my rolling

office chair

w/ my yellow sticky notes, my *Chicago Manual of Style,* my

soundproof carpeted cubicle and my Zip Drive and stapler and email and voicemail
and chainmail of paperclips

knew:

all words.

And it is, just.

They

are.

inkblot x's and o's, barbed hugs   AND   sticky black licorice kisses

sly and serifed on the plain vanilla pages,

spiky, sludge-marrowed
skeletons of blind birds
flailing across whitewashed sky,

They are maimed stick-figure storm troopers,
headless, starved tar babies named,
Lucida Casual, Courier:
       ab-
solutely arbitary
at
best

                                    containing no

                          meaning thems-

                                  elves, only skinny signs

                symbols, chunks of broken chain links

                          on the highways leading
        back to history, the first echo, the empty answer to people who

howled and grunted

at God, craved to be understood,

to ut-
ter something, to mouth the smoke ring vowels

                          of love,
to cough bloody
consonants in holocausts of silence,
                mere *suggestion*

their climax,
        (asymptotic, asynchronous, ascendant, aspirant, as if—)

        powerless, really, when you think   a-

bout it.
Hovering equivocal,
serried

        in mothball alphabets and indeces

        saying to us

they are

the nothing

        we   embrace

instead

           of the something

        we   could.

(Which is what I really wanted to say to you that day,

when I realized it,)

    almost picking up the phone, dialing . . . "Hello, I love you. Hey, listen . . . "

staring at the louvered shadows

shredding gray sunlight across my desk, the iridescent fly carcasses,

belly-up

        on the dust-caked sill, and the steady blue haze

  an open cover

  of

        June sky

above the city   that   gave me   my computer-printed pay-

    check every day

But I realized

then that my wish

        was my prison—

having conceived

of only *saying* it,

                        [the idea unexpressed rattling

    in my [heart] like

a
jar

        of dull hardware parts or glittering gulls swimming in

a giant drinking glass
of heaven,   the letters merely spelling out the desire, loud & brilliant]

that

    what I

wanted   [what I want now,

        when I'm with you]

      isn't

complete mastery

of

                                    but absolute freedom
    from

        all words!

Acknowledgments

American Aesthetic:	"On the Last Day of the Mayan Calendar"
ANIMAL: Writers in the Attic:	"A Presence"
	"Sonnet: Breed"
	"Trumpeter Swan/Beaver: 1/1/11"
Apeiron Review:	"The Cadenza"
	"Though"
Avatar Review:	"Death of a Fox"
	"A Small Thing"
Bateau:	"Still River"
The Cape Rock:	"Sixteena"
Cherry Tree:	"Soccer Dads"
Enchantment of the Ordinary:	"To People Who Talk to Themselves in Cars"
GAME: Writers in the Attic:	"Allen Iverson"
	"Ernest Hemingway Boxes Ezra Pound: A Primer"
Gyroscope Review:	"Shame and Guilt"
HA&L Magazine:	"Taking Goethe to the Eastern Idaho State Fair"
	"Tree as Lens"
The Healing Muse:	"The Last Time"
The Hopper:	"Short Discourse on Species"
Irreantum:	"The Dogs of Sligo"
Juxtaprose:	"In Keeping"
	"Maundy Thursday"
	"What Is a Crow?"
Lake Effect:	"November Gale (Skaneateles, New York, 1993)"
Mantra Review:	"Running in Trearddur Bay"
Mixed Fruit:	"To All Abandoned Cars"
Plume:	"At Once People at the End of Their Lives"
Quail Bell Magazine:	"We Are a World"
	"The Persian Legends"
	"Poem That Will Never Be Turned into a Summer Blockbuster"
	"Hidden Motion"
Open: Journal of Arts & Letters	"I Realized Today"
The Raw Art Review:	"In the Harriet Tubman Home"
Rougarou:	"What Is a Magpie?"
Shambles:	"What Is a Pelican?"

Slant:	"The Fool"
Soliloquies Anthology:	"The Poem of the Future"
	"Running in New Hope"
SONG: Writers in the Attic:	"American Anthem"
	"Hymn for the Control Freak"
South Florida Poetry Journal:	"What Is a Flamingo?"
Stoneboat:	"In All the Novels"
Sunset Liminal:	"We Are a Country"
	"Cruise Poem"
	"Home Movies"
Tilde:	"Pennsylvania Pantoum"
WATER: Writers in the Attic:	"Buoyancy"
	"Cycle"
	"Swimming in Buttermere"
Welter:	"Manent II"
West Trade Review:	"All Words"

Matthew James Babcock is the author of *Four Tales of Troubled Love* (fiction), *Heterodoxologies* (nonfiction), *Points of Reference* (poetry), *Strange Terrain* (poetry), and *Private Fire: The Ecopoetry and Prose of Robert Francis* (criticism). His awards include the Juxtaprose Poetry Prize, a Dorothy Sargent Rosenberg Poetry Award, the AML Poetry Award, the Next Generation Indie Book Award for Short Fiction, and Winner of Press 53's Open Awards Anthology Prize for his novella, *He Wanted to be a Cartoonist for* The New Yorker. He was born in San Francisco and lives with his family in Idaho.

www.ingramcontent.com/pod-product-compliance
Lightning Source LLC
Chambersburg PA
CBHW021149090426
42740CB00008B/1017